FRESHWATER
GAME FISH
OF NORTH AMERICA

FRESHWATER
GAME FISH
OF NORTH AMERICA

FRIEDMAN/FAIRFAX
PUBLISHERS

A FRIEDMAN/FAIRFAX BOOK

Library of Congress Cataloging-in-Publication Data

Schaffner, Herbert A.
    Freshwater game fish of North America / Herbert A. Schaffner.
        p. cm.
    Includes index.
    ISBN 1-56799-153-X (pbk.)
    1. Fishing—North America. 2. Freshwater fishes—North
America. I. Title.
SH462.S33   1995
799.1'1—dc20   94-27975
                                      CIP

Editor: Sharyn Rosart
Art Director: Jeff Batzli
Designer: Devorah H. Levinrad
Photography Editor: Christopher C. Bain
Photography Researcher: Ede Rothaus

All illustrations are by Ron Pittard © Windsor Publications, Inc., Eugene, Oregon
Typeset by Mar + X Myles
Color separations by United South Sea Graphic Art Co., Ltd.
Printed in China by Leefung-Asco Printers Ltd.

For bulk purchases and special sales, please contact:
Friedman/Fairfax Publishers
Attention: Sales Department
15 West 26th Street
New York, NY 10010
212/685-6610 FAX 212/685-1307

Acknowledgments

While I have much more to learn about the piscine universe, I would know even less without the guidance of my father, who made me a fisherman. Thanks, Dad. The companionship of many angling friends through the years was essential to my maturing angling abilities and enjoyment of the sport.

I must thank Tim Frew and Sharyn Rosart of the Michael Friedman Publishing Group. Tim got the project rolling with the right mixture of humor and enthusiasm, and Sharyn Rosart carefully guided the book to completion with encouragement and efficiency. She showed a nice sense of humor, too. Devorah Levinrad was a pleasure to work with, and learned quickly about fish and fish photography. Best of luck to them all.

Thanks from the heart to Laura Schenone, my wife, for computer time—and everything.

This book is dedicated to Andy McCormick, a good friend and very good writer.

PART 1

Introduction to Freshwater Game Fish

PART 2 Meet the Game Fish

Above all, perhaps, there is the direction of man

towards knowledge and intimate observation that would

otherwise escape him; knowledge of water and its

behavior, of fish, insects, and birds, as well as of animals

in their relation to one another.

—Roderick Haig-Brown, *The Western Angler*

Introduction

Watch any good trout pool on a warm spring evening. Fly-fishermen will line the banks and shallows, backcasting and stripping furiously as they work their piece of water. Keep watching. From this crowd of a dozen anglers or more, one or two will begin to stand out. These anglers are catching trout—striking, netting, and releasing. The others watch them with poorly guarded envy and furiously check flies, change leaders, and lengthen their casts. But they rarely change their luck. Perhaps during the major hatch of the afternoon, they will each catch a trout. But those few busy fly-fishermen will have already released a half dozen fish, and during the hatch they will land a half dozen more.

Or stand at a boat ramp on a large lake or reservoir where bass fishing is popular and chart the results of the anglers as they leave the water and load up their boats. Most of the anglers will have caught a few bass, but a few of them will have caught dozens, and most of them will be the first off the water, having caught their limit and decided to move on to other matters of the day.

If you talk to the "lucky" fly-fisherman or interview the "hot" bass angler, you will discover they have certain ...*understandings* in common as good fishermen. Perhaps the most important is this: They understand how fish behave. The fly-fisherman knows that the local brown trout feed on subsurface Hendrickson nymphs an hour or two before the hatch; the bass angler knows that large bass can be found in shallow cover when their spawning period has just concluded. The fly-fisherman knows that larger browns can be found on the windward bank of the stream where a stiff breeze is blowing freshly hatched mayflies into the water; the bass angler knows that his favorite variety of

Georgia bass gorges itself on the small perch easily available in the spring shallows, not the deep-water shad it favors later in the season. In fact, both fishermen could tell you so much about their favorite prey that you could write a book with all that you learned from them.

Indeed, the best fishermen are amateur ichthyologists with an unquenchable curiosity about the feeding, mating, migrating, and territorial habits of their prey. This book offers a complete freshman seminar on the lives and loves of America's top game fish, whether they swim in the Great Lakes of the Midwest or the huge reservoir systems of the South. You'll learn the fundamentals of catching and the fine points of identifying a wealth of species in their native habitats. Here is information on where fish can be found in local waters over the course of the year and which lures, baits, flies, and rigs are most effective for different days— and *times* of day. You'll discover where the fish live naturally and where different species have been successfully transplanted through the aggressive fisheries management of federal and local authorities.

This book also takes you beneath the watery surface to tell you why fish live the way they do—their mating, migratory, and feeding habits. Fish are sport to the angler, a desired object, but *they* don't know that. To them, their environment is the entire universe, and our interfering with it makes no instinctive sense except that our presence disturbs or frightens them. From the fish's perspective, fishing does not exist. This book makes an attempt to share a little of the fish's point of view, while understanding the angler's full well. Remember: The more you know about your prey, the more and larger fish you will catch.

Introduction to Freshwater Game Fish

PA

The Making of a Freshwater Game Fish

While there are over twenty-five thousand known species of fish worldwide, about twenty thousand of those species live in salt water. Of the five thousand or so freshwater species, only a few thousand occur in North America. And of those minnows, guppies, panfish, bottom feeders, and predators, only about thirty species of game fish have earned the interest of the North American angler.

You know the stars of the game fish world. The trout, pike, bass, walleye, salmon, and catfish lure eager legions to the banks and boats of local watersheds. But there are more furtive breeds, elusive champions obsessively pursued by the cultish sportsman or the local devotee. Such salmonids as the Apache trout, Kamloops trout, Kokanee salmon, and golden trout have many admirers. Bottom fishing for carp and buffalo is considered an art by some anglers; a predator named the gar enjoys some angler attention, as do the lowly perch, which travel in eager masses, and the wildly compliant crappie, suicidal attacker of jigs and spoons.

In any freshwater habitat, the various riparian life-forms perform one of four roles in the food chain. *Consumers* are the crayfish, minnows, and other underwater animal life forms that feed strictly on plants and plankton. *Foragers,* such as perch, sunfish, bluegills, and small bass and trout, eat the consumers and sometimes plankton. Bass, trout, pike, walleye, and a few other species are established as *predators* after a year or so of growth. They prey on the foragers, insects, and crustaceans, but are still vulnerable to bears, heron, eagles, and other predators outside of the riparian habitat. Other game fish are *bottom feeders*—carp, buffalo, catfish—working the river or lake bottom for buried vegetation.

Kokanee salmon

Different predators forage at different water levels. The lake trout is a consistently deep-swimming fish, inhabiting the lower thermocline (the oxygen-rich middle layer in a body of still water favored by most fish), while the walleye devours fish and other slimy creatures on river or lake bottom. Largemouth bass, however, are well known to anglers as top-water hunters that prowl lily pads and shorelines not only for careless salamanders and frogs, but also for mice and other shore creatures that wander down by the water for a drink.

Ichthyologists classify all fish into two huge groups, based on a fundamental anatomical distinction. The *cartilaginous* fish evolved to have skeletons made only of cartilage; these species, primarily sharks, skates, and rays, are

largely found in salt water. In most cartilaginous species, the eggs of the female are fertilized and hatched within her body and born alive. The skates, however, drop their eggs in the sea within a tough sealed pouch. Cartilaginous fish must swim or sink, as they lack the air bladder that allows the other major group of fish to regulate the depth at which they swim.

Most freshwater fish are *bony*—that is, their skeletons are made of bone. In addition, bony fish are distinguished from the cartilaginous fish by their behavior. The bony fish hatch their young outside the body in eggs that are expelled and fertilized in nests, or *redds,* or simply dropped into open water or over sandy or rocky bottoms. All bony fish have air bladders. The respiratory systems of bony and car-

tilaginous fish are quite similar, except that most bony fish evolved to have gill *plates* rather than the gill *slits* of sharks and rays.

Many anglers and nature lovers know that salmon and other trout will move out to the ocean for long periods to feed and live, eventually returning to the freshwater rivers of their birth to spawn, where people with expensive rods and fancy flies will be waiting patiently to figure out how to catch these sex-crazed fish. This rather familiar *anadromous* behavior contrasts with the more obscure *catadromous* fish, such as the American eel and barramundi. These travel from saltwater birthplaces to live in freshwater streams and rivers and then return to their saltwater birthing grounds to spawn.

They Came to Their Senses

Fish live in a fluid, highly pressurized environment where predators and prey live and move in close proximity, competition for the best food and shelter is high, and feeding opportunities are strictly limited by the dimensions and condition of the environment. Survival requires that fish have highly refined senses, and nothing so impresses us about the fish's extraordinary adaptability of function to habitat than its sensory capabilities.

Most predator fish possess strong eyesight, and ichthyologists agree that bass, pike, trout, and other fresh and saltwater fish can discern color. Studies have established that certain lure color patterns draw more strikes than others from particular game fish. Gary Soucie quotes a study in *Hook, Line & Sinker* that states black bass will hit red lures more than any other color. Jim Maxwell, formerly of Grizzly Tackle, found that in tests of about a thousand fish of each species, ninety-four percent of the lake trout he caught hit lures finished in silver, pearl, chartreuse, or combinations of these colors; eighty-six percent of the steelhead caught hit pink, red, or orange with combinations of silver and pearl; and seventy-seven percent of brown trout preferred brass- or copper-finished lures.

The vibrancy of color lessens in deeper and dimmer waters, losing varying degrees of visibility as *color* to fish. Interestingly enough, red fades the fastest in deeper water, losing most of its hue in ten feet of water depth. Blue and green fare the best in deeper water, retaining large percentages of color visibility even in thirty or more feet of water.

Yellow and green lures offer a higher percentage of visibility underwater.

Accordingly, light lessens in freshwater habitats—when the sun goes down—red is the first color fish lose sight of; blue and green are the last. When the sun comes up and light enters their world, blue and green are the first colors fish will see, red the last. Examine the following table:

PERCENTAGES OF COLOR VISIBILITY UNDERWATER

Color	Percentages of visibility (%)		
	10 feet	*20 feet*	*30 feet*
RED	6.5	.4	.025
ORANGE	50	25	12
YELLOW	73	53	40
GREEN	88	78	69

Since red and other colors fade to shades of gray and black only a short distance underwater, it seems that color density and pattern may often trigger the predating response. Many fish, however, can see ultraviolet colors invisible to the human eye. At the Woods Hole Marine Biological Laboratory in Massachusetts, researchers discovered that the Japanese dace, *Tribolodon hakonensis,* can see very shortwave ultraviolet color invisible to human beings. A scan of colors at this end of the spectrum revealed that each fish bears two stripes on its belly that may help dace recognize each other. Fish do communicate through color patterns. When a bluefish female is ready to mate, a bright inflamed spot emerges behind its pectoral fin, the sight of which inflames the ardor of male blues. John Hersey in his classic *Blues* says this about the eyes of blues and other fish:

> The biggest difference, of course, and to us the creepiest one, is that the eyes are on the sides of the fish's head, so it can see almost all around. Like having eyes where our ears are. . . . Each bluefish eye is independent of the other—can wobble about to look in one direction on one side, and quite another on the other. I get woozy talking about it.

Trout, bass, pike, and walleye possess excellent vision, even at night. This is of course crucial to their ability to

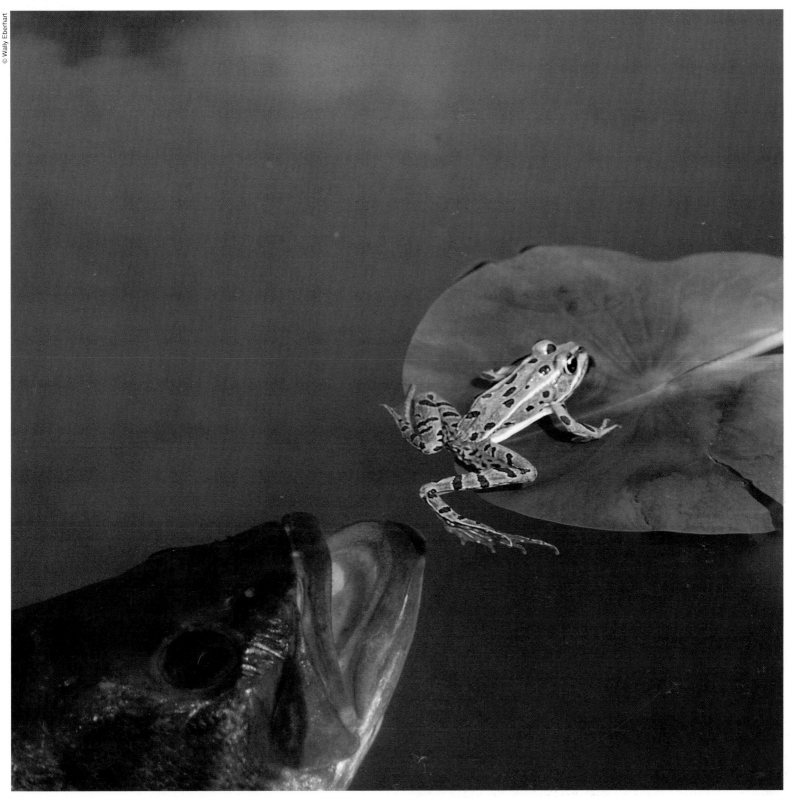

Largemouth bass possess excellent vision, and from a deep hold can see small objects and potential prey on the water's surface.

© Daniel W. Gotshall

The fish's lateral line senses the vibrations of artificial lures, which the gamefish—a walleye (left), and rainbow trout (above)—often interpret to be wounded prey.

find and attack prey—and avoid danger. Many a frustrated fly-fisherman can tell you about the vision of trout, which can pick up thin strands of leader, faint ripples of dragging flies, slightly damaged fly hackle, and other minutiae that turn hungry trout away from a floating fly. Studies have cited the ability of pike to pick out small nocturnal water creatures on the surface up to twenty-five feet away. Often predators will pick up the "warning signals" and water disturbances of struggling or wounded bait fish through their lateral line, circle closer for inspection, and then lock on the prey visually to make the kill.

Sound travels five times faster in water than air, and fish are equipped with a number of sound- and vibration-detection "devices." A fish's *lateral line* is a thin horizontal stripe of open pores that acts as a combination sense, encompassing hearing, touch, and a kind of indefinable radar. It provides what has been called "a sense of distant touch." The pores act as an extremely sensitive set of receptors that detect the slightest vibrations in the surrounding water, whether generated by the movement of other fish, noise, or waves. Fish can therefore respond to movements toward or away from them in any direction, including their blind spots in the rear and under their nose. Ichthyologists speculate that the lateral line allows schooling fish to orient themselves in relation to one another, therefore creating the

most efficient movement possible through the water for each fish. The lateral line also makes it possible for fish to move, attack, and hide at night as well as they do. The *swim bladder,* present in all bony fish, not only regulates their swimming depth, but acts as a detector of sound pressure and waves—at higher frequencies and farther distances (though it does not sense the direction from which the waves are generated) than the lateral line, complementing it to form a complete detector system. In some catfish, a small bone chain called the *Weberian apparatus* connects the swim bladder to the inner ear, providing these fish with an extremely acute "sense of hearing."

All fish possess an inner ear that is remarkably similar to that of mammals and other vertebrates, composed of three semicircular canals, which serve the equilibrium sense and the otolith organs. In other words, the inner ear helps fish keep their "balance" and swim right side up in water where no light or other stimuli provide visual cues.

The powers of piscine smell are, in general, extraordinary. Salmon can detect one part per billion of odorous material in water. They will not use fish ladders in which human hands or bear paws were dipped in the running water. Salmon exhibited panic activity in swimming pools in which *one drop* of bear-scented water was released.

Salmon, trout, and other anadromous fish "home in"

Anglers patrolling Florida's Lake Okeechobee.

◀ *A sinking plug took this beauty.* ▲ *A collection of "Mr. Mean" plastic lures from Cabela's.*

hawg. Hooked under the dorsal fin and weighted with tiny split shot or, conversely, suspended under a bobber and cast near weed beds and lily pads, shiners and minnows will draw voracious strikes even when artificials are not productive. Live crayfish, salamanders, and water dogs will also draw lively interest. Generally, live bait is less effective when probing for largemouth holds, because you can't cover large sections of water; bait rigs are best for those particular spots where you have already found fish.

Flies   Bass hit streamers and wet flies when active in the shallows and near riverbanks. Bass popper flies are extremely popular with bass busters and fly-fishermen alike when the big guys are cruising the surface. Dave Whitlock's frog, bug, and mouse patterns are pop-

ular, as are the Bumble Bee Diver, Black Bug, Bullfrog Popper, Water Tickler, Fat Gnat, Dynamite, Sneaky Pete, Dixie Devil, and Bass Duster, among hundreds of bug patterns.

Best tackle   The casting accuracy (thumb pressure drops the lure where you want it) and cranking power of bait-casting reels have made them the foundation of bass tackle outfits, especially as antibraking and antireverse technology have made the reels easier to use. A 7- to 8-foot bait-casting rod and lightweight bait-casting reel fitted with 8- to 10-pound test to ease tough retrieves through weeds and cover will serve the bass angler in most shoreline and structure lake fishing. Where casting distance is crucial to cover large stretches of moving river, spinning tackle in light and medium-light classes will extend range.

SMALLMOUTH BASS

*I*t is a highly prized sport fish in cool water fisheries over all of its range. The magnitude, antiquity, and intensity of interest in the smallmouth is reflected in the fact that angling results were mentioned in Fothergill's 1816 to 1836 "account of the natural history of eastern Canada."

—William F. Sigler and John W. Sigler, *Fishes of the Great Basin*

SMALLMOUTH BASS

Range Native to the eastern half of the United States and southeastern Canada, from Manitoba and Quebec south to the Tennessee River system, the smallmouth has been successfully stocked continent-wide. It is not, however, found in as many places as the largemouth. The smallmouth prefers cool, clean rivers with rocky or gravelly bottoms and deep, cool, rocky lakes. It will not feed in water warmer than 80°F.

Color The smallmouth is golden bronze or brown with a cream belly (in contrast to the greenish color of largemouth bass) and has dark vertical marks or bands on its flanks, with a dash of red in its eyes.

Identifying characteristics

The smallmouth's jaw extends directly below, not beyond, the eye, and his cheeks have twelve to seventeen rows of scales. The dorsal fins are joined with ten spines and thirteen to fourteen soft rays.

Size

Most smalls weigh between 1 and 1.5 pounds, but they can run as high as 4 or 5 pounds as they grow to a maximum age of about ten years. The all-tackle smallmouth world record is an 11-pound, 15-ounce fish caught in Kentucky in 1955.

Spawning period

Smallmouths prefer water temperatures between 62° and 65° F for spawning, which usually occurs between April and June. They will move into the shallows of lakes or streams in water depths between 2 and 10 feet. The male smallmouth sweeps debris from a small area to create a gravelly spawning bed. The male remains to guard the nest after spawning until the fry are freely swimming at about one month or so.

Angling notes

Migration and schooling habits differ between lake and river smallmouths, especially in seasonal habitat changes. In still or moving waters, smallmouths move from habitat to habitat as the temperature changes over the course of a year. Smallmouths prefer cool water, but will follow food sources. The angler is forewarned to analyze each angling situation according to weather, water quality, food availability, and surface-feeding activity.

An angler lands a smallmouth on Minnesota's Boundary Waters.

The river smallmouth will linger in shallow rocky pools and ledges during cooler spring weather and then move to the edges of the river's main channel and on to deeper, slow-current pools as the temperature heats up. The smallmouth feeds in water between 60° and 70° F. Bedrock and sand-covered-bottom habitats are generally avoided by smalls, since little aquatic food can be found in these barren areas. Smallmouths prefer coarse, gravelly bottoms, slab rock edifices where forage is plentiful, weedy patches, and other crayfish and minnow hangouts. Generally, habitats that yield bass in one part of the river will also yield bass in other parts: If you catch a smallmouth in a deep pool off the current, concentrate on fishing similar areas throughout the river. Cast carefully and quietly to likely pools, and be patient; often smalls will follow a lure for a number of retrieves before striking. Smallmouths are easily spooked and should be approached with care. Wading anglers should make a minimum of noise and watch where their shadows fall.

In lakes, smallmouths follow the same general pattern, moving to deeper water as the weather heats up, schooling and holding in deep pockets and around structure and shade. Offshore, they favor sunken bars and reefs, submerged islands, rocky points, drop-offs, and ledges. Smallmouths school in deeper waters around weed and grass beds, where minnows, crayfish, and other favorite foods are available.

Leading North American smallmouth waters include the James and Shenandoah rivers in Virginia; the Susquehanna River in Pennsylvania; Grand Lake, Rainy Lake, Baskahegan Lake, and others in Maine; the St. Lawrence River and St. Lawrence Islands National Park in Ontario; the Great Lakes; and other rocky-bottomed rivers and lakes.

Younger smalls are delicious.

© Marvin L. Dembinsky Jr.

Plugs and lures

In rivers, try poppers and chuggers near cool, shadowy shore water and cover. Small swimming plugs—such as the Storm Shiner Minnow, Rapala Minnow, Heddon Lucky 13, and Helin Fishcake—will take smalls off rocky river ledges and "steps," where they like to hide in spring and early summer. Spinners and spoons are effective when smallmouths are active in shallower river water during June and September—Mepps and Panther Martin, Johnson and Phoebe spoons and spinners will take plenty of smallmouths in these conditions. Try a variety of jigs when they move deep in hot weather, such as the Gaines Wiggle or Betts Krinkle jigs tipped with pork rind. Small dark crankbaits (Shad Rap, Natural Ike), crayfish imitators, and spinners are also worth trying near the bottom of pools, currents, and riffles.

In lakes, spoons and spinners are deadly in still water when fishing the

Tireless fighters, smallmouths are electrifying sport on a fly rod.

shallows for active fish. Crankbaits, larger spinners, and small trolling plugs yield the best results when smallmouths move into deep lake water for the summer. Jigs are terrific lures for the deep-water smallmouth: No lure is more efficient when you know where the fish are hiding. Add a strip of pork rind or a plastic worm if the fish are reluctant. Try bucktails, streamers, spoons, and spinners around structure—such as rocks, docks, logs, overhanging branches, pilings, and ledges—during the morning and late afternoon, especially in spring.

Bait Smallmouth anglers often favor live crayfish or minnows in deep lake water, hooked with a small split shot to get them to the bottom. Hellgrammites are deadly in streams and rivers, and even worms will catch smalls if you know where they are feeding. If you're fishing a lake, try casting your worm, hellgrammite, or minnow rig into shallow water around structure. Frogs, crayfish,

A gorgeous specimen.

The aggressive, never-say-die smallmouth can make for an exciting afternoon when stalked on the fly rod.

crickets, and salamanders are also terrific baits when fished around structure —since this is where these creatures live and are found by predatory fish.

Flies   Popping plugs, streamers, and bucktails are usually effective on smallmouths during cool-water months. They will hit dry flies when a hatch is on and take bugs and streamers in the shallows and at tails of pools. Try slowly trolling streamers, such as the marabou, sculpin, or Muddler, around drop-offs, and submerged and above-water structure where smalls like to forage. You may find unforgettable action.

Best tackle   Without question, the top tackle for catching smallmouths with plugs and spinners is ultralight or light spinning equipment. The sensitivity of the rod allows the angler to feel soft small-

mouth taps of jigs and live bait. It also facilitates the short-range precision casting often required to work bass hot spots. Spinning reels offer better casting range as the smallmouth angler works a variety of water habitats to find individual smallmouths. Unlike largemouths, which prefer the same sort of structure houses time after time, smallmouths are more mobile, moving from pool to riffle to structure as they follow cool water and food.

When roaming the shallows, smallmouths are prime targets for the fly rod and offer electrifying action. While the largemouth bass bug angler must use a long rod to cast wind-resistant bass bugs to the hawgs, the smallmouth specialist can work with much lighter tackle—8- or 8.5-foot rods built for 6-weight line, coupled with a small stream reel and a light leader.

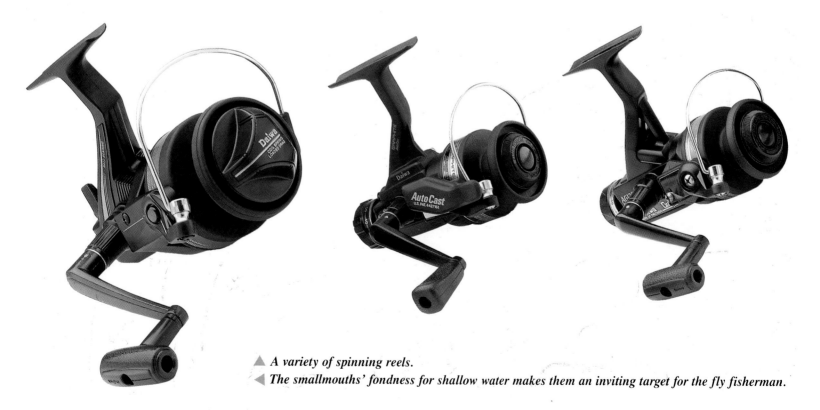

▲ *A variety of spinning reels.*
◀ *The smallmouths' fondness for shallow water makes them an inviting target for the fly fisherman.*

CATFISH AND BULLHEADS

*O*f all the members of the catfish family, bullheads are the most tolerant of water pollution, turbidity, and lack of oxygen. In ponds all but devoid of oxygen, I have seen them cruising the surface, taking their oxygen directly from the air, and as a kid I dug bullheads from dry pond bottoms that looked like a huge puzzle of cracked earth. Under those conditions the fish were in the center of large lumps of dried mud. When the lump opened it was similar to breaking an egg; each bullhead had constructed a small cell slightly larger than its body and lined with a mucuslike substance from the skin of the fish. The substance apparently allowed air into the lump but did not allow the interior moisture to evaporate. When dropped into the water, these bullheads immediately swam away, apparently unharmed by many weeks without water.

—Mike Rosenthal, *North America's Freshwater Fishing Book*

CHANNEL CATFISH

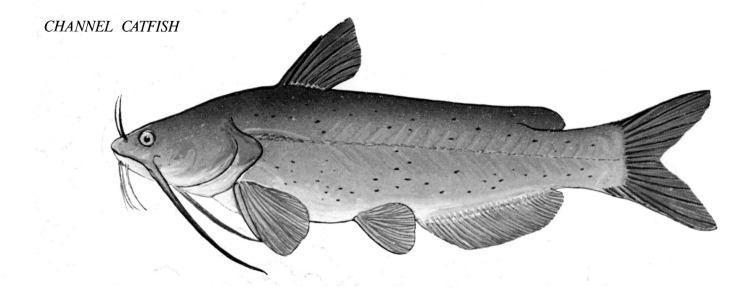

BULLHEAD

The popularity of the catfish species with bottom fishermen and their excellent qualifications for the table make them one of America's top recreational fish.

Range Four species of cats receive the attention of bottom fishermen.

Bullheads are found from the great Lakes to Florida and from New York and Pennsylvania west to the Rocky Mountains. *Channel catfish* are distributed over most of the United States and lower Canada, as far north as southern Canada and as far west as the Rockies. They prefer large, clean lakes and rivers. They can live in virtually any body of water, however, no matter how warm or chemically degraded. The *flathead catfish* is well established in the rivers of the Mississippi Valley and other waters of the Midwest, as well as in western Pennsylvania, southwestern Wisconsin, South Dakota, and northern Texas. These cats are found in large bodies of water, from reservoirs to big rivers. The *blue catfish* ranges over most of the Midwest and the South, as well as in northern Mexico. It prefers large, clear, silt-bottomed, free-flowing rivers.

Color Brown bullheads have a brown mottled back and flanks fading to an off-white belly. Black bullheads are green to black on the back with pale flanks and a white or yellow belly. The channel catfish has a slender body and a silver-

Discovering a pod of hungry catfish will provide the angler with a full afternoon of fishing.

FLATHEAD CATFISH

BLUE CATFISH

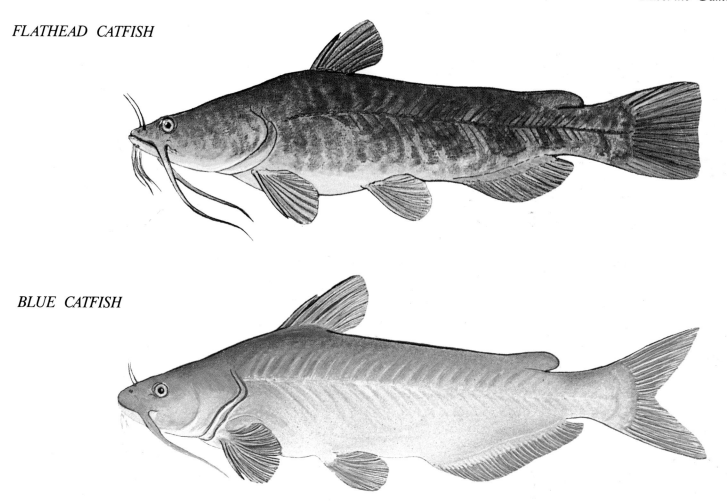

blue or olive back that slopes to pale flanks and a silvery white belly. It is covered with a handful of black spots. Flathead catfish are olive-yellow to light brown on the back and sides, with yellow and brown spots and a yellowish white belly. Blue catfish have gray, dusky blue backs with a silvery white belly and deeply forked tails.

Identifying characteristics The bullheads are distinguishable from other cats by their rounded tail. Channel cats have distinctly forked tails and are liberally spotted. Flathead cats also have a rounded tail, but their heads are noticeably flatter and their bodies are

sleeker and thinner than the bullhead's. Blue cats have a deeply forked tail and distinctive blue coloration and are the largest of the freshwater cats.

Spawning period All catfish and bullheads spawn in May, June, and July, in water between 60° and 70° F.

Size The blue is the largest North American freshwater catfish, growing to disturbing, even nightmarish sizes of 100 to 110 pounds, and the average blue weighs between 35 and 50 pounds! Stories abound of landed blues breaking apart boats or "green" fish snapping poles or

ALL-TACKLE WORLD RECORDS

Brown bullhead:
5 pounds 8 ounces; Veal Pond/Georgia 1975

Black bullhead:
8 pounds; Lake Waccabuc/New York 1951

Blue catfish:
109 pounds, 4 ounces; Cooper River/South Carolina 1991

Channel catfish:
58 pounds; Santee-Copper Reserve/South Carolina 1964

Flathead catfish:
91 pounds, 4 ounces; Lake Lewisville/Texas 1982

pulling anglers into the water. Channel cats have been caught that are as large as 40 and 50 pounds, but the average size falls between 3 and 5 pounds, though they mutate to much bigger sizes down South. The flathead catfish shows the widest weight range in adult cats, topping out at 5 pounds up North but filling out nicely to sea-monster proportions of 80 or more pounds down in the slow, warm Southern waters.

Angling notes Catfish and bullheads are extraordinarily hardy fish that represent one of the finer achievements of evolution. Their staggering adaptability spans a great range of temperatures and water conditions. In fact, digestive enzymes in the catfish belly double their action for every eight-degree increase in water temperature: As the water gets hotter, cats get hungrier. Bullheads and other cats can survive with little oxygenated water—in fact, often with very little water at all.

Catfish, notorious bottom feeders and "garbage cleaners," respond best to baits that trigger their olfactory sense; however, more aggressive individuals will hit spinners, lures, or an occasional fly. Serious catfish anglers have had the most success with these baits and lures:

Bullheads: Stink baits, earthworms, crawfish, corn, cheese, and pork-rind-tipped jigs

Flathead catfish: Live suckers, minnows, crawfish, grasshoppers, shrimp, cut shad, and large pork rinds

Blue catfish: Live suckers and small carp, other live fish, clusters of shrimp and leeches, frogs, salamanders, and water dogs

Channel catfish: Worms, cheese, dough balls, grubs, marshmallows, cut shad or chub, and live minnows fished in the current or along the bottom.

Catfish are bottom-feeders, and that's where you must fish to catch them. Here catfish anglers wait out a fall day in Minnesota.

ARCTIC CHAR AND DOLLY VARDEN

A char taken on a fly typically moves with rapierlike speed for about one hundred feet, then leaps clear of the water and runs again. A four- or five-pound fish jumps a half-dozen times in swift currents and goes well down into the backing before it can be turned.

—A.J. McClane

ARCTIC CHAR

Range The most northerly of all freshwater fish, the arctic char and Dolly Varden are two virtually indistinguishable members of the char clan in the salmonid family that live in the northern reaches of New England in the United States and range northward through Canada, Alaska, and the Aleutian Islands. Few anglers can positively distinguish between the two species, and both are beautiful, plentiful, and extremely hard-fighting game fish that are not easily accessible but are highly desired. Both species are anadromous, moving out to sea as adults and returning to freshwater to spawn.

Color   In fresh water, the char and Dolly Varden have electric-bright flanks striped with pink and brilliant red, green and blue on top and coated with cream-colored spots from head to toe. As with all char, the leading edge of their fins is coated in white. Sea-going "steelhead" char and Dolly Varden are fitted in silver, flashing mail with few spots.

Identifying characteristics   Few positive methods of distinguishing between these two species are available.

The angler can try to count the gill rakers: Char have twenty-five to thirty gill rakers; Dolly Varden have twenty-one to twenty-two. Char have forty to forty-five *pyloric caeca* (tubular patches opening into the alimentary canal); Dolly Varden have around thirty. But, of course, counting pyloric caeca requires cutting open the fish, which isn't all that healthy for those fish you would like to return to their ancestral waters. Often, the flank spots on the pre-sea-run char are larger than those of the Dolly Varden, but spawning fish lose their spots entirely. Size is a good indicator in much larger fish, because it is generally agreed that Dolly Varden

© Ruth Fairall

In pursuit of Dolly Varden in Alaska.

Inuit fishermen with two sea-run Arctic char.

DOLLY VARDEN (Coastal Form)

rarely weigh more than 10 pounds. Guides and local experts can be helpful in identifying which species are more common in local watersheds and in pointing out regional identifying characteristics.

Size

Preocean adult char and Dolly Varden commonly weigh between 2 and 5 pounds, depending on forage availability. Field research tells us that the arctic char runs much larger in older years, after migrating to the ocean. Sea-run char of 10 to 20 pounds are often caught, while few positively identified Dolly Varden have weighed over 10 pounds. The world record arctic char was caught in Tree River, Canada in 1981 and tipped the scales at 32 pounds, 9 ounces. The top Dolly Varden specimen, taken from the Mashutuk River, Alaska weighed in at 18 pounds, 9 ounces.

Spawning period

Both species are anadromous spawners, returning to the rivers and streams of their birth to mate in early and late fall, when water temperatures drop below 40° F. Many of the adults of both species survive spawning and run to sea two or even three times.

Angling notes

Serious anglers—and you have to be to catch these two species—spend large sums of money and endure miserable weather to add the name "arctic char" to the list of game fish they can claim to have caught. The char reigns for serious trout fishermen and fly-rodders as a prize species of enormous mystique. It reaches large sizes and is a beautiful salmonid. The char is a willing strike and ferocious fighter. Most of all, it is a fish that requires the angler to understand the forbidding, mysterious arctic environment and its supreme challenges of weather and distance.

Fly fishing

The char responds to salmon egg baits, both real and imitation. Brightly colored spinners and spoons are the foundation of spinning techniques for both species. Fly fishers prefer the larger orange and red streamers and wet flies popular for salmon and steelhead as well as char. Favorite patterns include Orange Babine, Alaskabous in various colors, Comet, Thor, Roe patterns, and Zonkers.

CRAPPIES

CRAPPIE

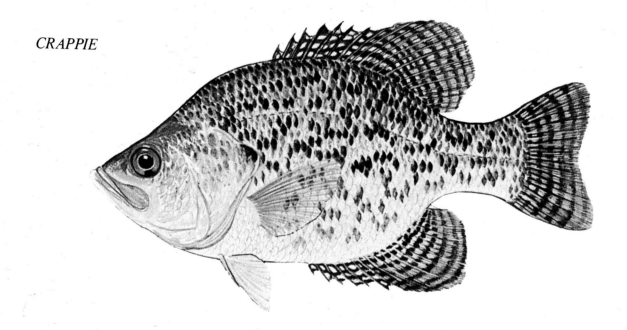

Range

Plentiful, easy to catch, and tasty at the table, the crappie is America's panfish for the masses. The *black (Pomoxis nigromaculatus)* and *white (P. annularis) crappies* are found in huge numbers from Canada to Mexico, as far west as the Great Plains and as far east as New York. The black crappie has been transplanted into some Rocky Mountain states, and the white crappie has been extensively stocked throughout the western and southwestern border states. The white crappie has also been introduced with some success in New England and coastal southern states. Where food is available, the crappie inevitably thrives, multiplying to a point of overpopulation in two or three years.

As more fish compete for less forage in the habitat, cannibalism of fry will begin, cutting the number of adult crappies until bait fish regenerate.

Color

The black and white crappie are almost identical in coloration. From the spine to the lateral line, both are dark olive or brownish black and flecked with silver. Their lower flanks are silverish and their entire bodies—including the dorsal, anal, and pectoral fins—are mottled with blackish spots. Spotting patterns are distinctly different in black and white crappies. The white crappie's spots are lighter and neatly arranged in seven to nine vertical rows, while spotting on the black crappie is heavier and

Crappies will move to deep water in summer.

ATLANTIC SALMON

The salmon is anadromous. That is to say, he leads a double life, one of them in freshwater, the other in saltwater. His freshwater life may be said to be his private, or love life; his saltwater life his ordinary, or workaday life. The salmon reverses the common order of human affairs: a lot is known about his private life but nothing at all about the rest. We get the chance to study him only when the salmon is making love.

—William Humphrey, *The Spawning Run*

ATLANTIC SALMON

Range The Atlantic salmon, the famous *Salmo salar*, is, as Mr. Humphrey mentions, an anadromous fish. Spawned in rivers of the northeastern United States, Canada, and Europe, Atlantic salmon remain as *parr* in their rivers of birth for at least two and sometimes as many as five years. Then called *smolt*, they migrate to the open waters of the Atlantic, where they school with other salmon in huge ocean feeding grounds off Greenland and Norway. While aggressive commercial overfishing in these waters has often posed a severe threat to Atlantic salmon populations, a recent government buyout of commercial fishing licenses in these areas has greatly reduced this danger. At different periods for different classes of fish during this two- to five-year period at open sea, Atlantic salmon will begin to journey back to the rivers of their birth to spawn. Salmon are listed as freshwater fish because, in North America, they are fished primarily with rod and reel when they return to spawn in the freshwater rivers of Nova Scotia, Maine, New Brunswick, Quebec, and Newfoundland.

Most Atlantic salmon die after upriver spawning, but some live to return to the sea and begin again the cycle of growth, strength, and the struggle to return. Some of the surviving salmon remain in their spawning rivers as *kelts*, or black salmon, as they are sometimes called. After surviving the winter in a state of very low metabolism, the kelts launch an all-out campaign to rebuild strength and begin to feed voraciously. These gaunt, nearly wasted fish don't make much of a meal and offer little challenge to the angler since they are so hungry after the exhaustions of the fall and winter that they eat everything in their path. When hooked, a kelt often expends nearly all its remaining energy fighting the angler; in cases like this, even if the kelt is released quickly, it will probably die. But kelts left to forage and return to the sea will arrive next year on the river at world record sizes, fattened, healthy, and "bright" from a year of feeding at sea. Smart anglers don't fish for black salmon—it's that simple.

Color

The bright adult salmon fresh from the sea is green-blue on the back with sil-

Atlantic salmon in North America may be pursued only with fly tackle. A 9-foot rod matched with a heavy reel that can handle 8- or 9-weight line is a good combination for larger salmon.

very flanks and a white belly. As salmon approach the spawning stage, the lower jaw develops a hook, or *kype*, skin colors darken, taking on a pink hue, and its full body is marked with spots of red or black.

Identifying characteristics

The Atlantic salmon has a single dorsal fin and small, sharp teeth in the jaw. In prespawning salmon the jaw is hooked. The Atlantic salmon looks a great deal like the brown trout, but a number of characteristics distinguish them: The brown trout's spots are often "haloed" with red or white, unlike the Atlantic salmon's "plain" black spots; the brown has two rows of vomerine teeth (on the roof of the mouth), compared to one for the salmon; and the caudal fin of the Atlantic salmon is concave to square, while the brown's is fan shaped.

Size

Some salmon spend only one year in the open sea and return to their home rivers to spawn. These youngish, 3- and 4-pound salmon are called *grilse*. The adult salmon that return after two or three years generally weigh between 10 and 20 pounds. Any salmon caught on a fly rod weighing over 20 pounds is a champion, and 30-pounders are caught every once in a long while. Large, fast rivers like the Restigouche in Canada attract a larger run of salmon and 30-pounders are more common. The rod-and-reel record is a 79-pound, 2-ounce salmon, caught by Henrik Henriksen in Norway.

Spawning period

Atlantic salmon begin returning to freshwater rivers and streams in the spring of their spawning year. The earliest to return are the "bright" salmon. Runs continue through the summer and early fall as the stragglers enter fresh water and swim the final stage of their journey. By late fall of that year, salmon are spawning in the upper reaches of their parent rivers and streams.

Angling notes

No game fish has inspired greater interest, respect, and reverence through history than the Atlantic salmon. Eighteen hundred years ago, Pliny wrote: "In Aquitania the river salmon surpasseth all the fishes of the sea." Prized by the ancient Romans, both sought and protected for centuries by British anglers, hunted continually by the American Indian and his nemesis, the Colonial American, for whom the salmon was a dietary staple, this noble fish, with its sleek silver armor, has inspired profound angling desire wherever it has returned for freshwater spawning.

Today, it is illegal to fish for Atlantic salmon in North America with anything but a fly rod and reel. Salmon stop eating once they begin their spawning run. The history of salmon fly-tying has been shaped by tying-bench and field experiments that established which colors, patterns, and retrieves induce, annoy, irritate, or tempt the homing salmon into striking. Of course, a great deal of the responsibility for drawing the strike depends on the angler's skill in reading the attitude of the fish and presenting the fly in a way that attracts the attention of the highly preoccupied *S. salar*.

When the river waters are clear and warm, Atlantic salmon will occasionally rise to dry flies, such as the Wilkinson, Grey Wulff, Pink Lady, Irresistible, and Mackintosh. Most of the time, wet flies and streamers are more productive in the deep, fast-running rivers of Canada, to which most Atlantic salmon return. The salmon fisherman should keep an assortment of flies in a vest pocket— some hair-wings (drabber "modern" salmon flies tied with hair rather than feathers), some of the traditional, gaudily colored fancy salmon flies, and an assortment of bucktails and streamers.

In North America, salmon fishing begins as early as May on Maine's Penobscot River and as late as July on Ungava Bay in Quebec. Top salmon rivers include the Restigouche, Grand Cascapedia, Matapedia, Moisie, and the most famous of all, the Miramichi. In the early deep and fast runoff river water of May and June, large No. 2/0 and 3/0 wet salmon flies are recommended, fished deeply with stout leaders. As the season progresses, river levels drop and the water warms, and smaller flies and tippets can be worked more closely to the surface.

Salmon anglers generally agree that

Salmon are caught in the great pine forests and dark hills of Nova Scotia, Newfoundland, Quebec, and New Brunswick.

brighter flies work better in discolored water or under dark skies, and darker, drabber flies get more attention when the weather is clear and bright. When water visibility is good and the temperature is warm, the bright salmon will rise to a dry fly—one of the most spectacular sights in all of sport. The classic salmon approach is a cross- and downstream cast at a 45-degree angle, mended to pick up slack so the fly drifts naturally by the salmon's nose, picking up speed as the arc of the drift tightens with the speed of the current. As the fly completes the swing downstream, the rod should be lifted in the event a salmon strikes before pickup, allowing the angler to drop the rod tip and begin to play the fish. The fly should drift so that the salmon sees the entire side of the fly as it flattens out and begins to move away from it. This presentation is generally regarded as the most likely inducer of strikes.

In *Fishing the Big Three*, the great Ted Williams estimates that he makes three hundred to four hundred casts for each salmon he catches, and Williams has caught more fish on the Miramichi than anyone. Many dedicated salmon anglers fish for days without as much as a roll or a strike. Fishing for Atlantic salmon has often been branded a sport of the aristocracy, and certainly a large reason for this lies in the enormous amount of time required to catch even a single fish: Only the independently wealthy have the time to pursue it successfully. Still, the extraordinary qualities of the salmon and the satisfaction of landing one are so great that many recreational anglers pursue the sport in their spare time.

Because the Atlantic salmon is difficult to find, difficult to hook once you've found it, and difficult to land once you've hooked the fish, it is a good idea to enlist the services of a guide for your first trip to New Brunswick or Maine. A guide will save you an enormous amount of frustration as you spend day after day flailing the river without seeing a fish or even a rise. Once you've laid your salmon out on the grass, you'll never worry about the money you paid for the guide.

Best tackle

In *Fishing the Big Three*, Ted Williams recommends this range of fly tackle: an 8.5-foot fly rod that casts 9-weight line or a 9-foot rod in heavy wind, with a salmon reel holding 8- or 9-weight line as well as 150 yards of 30-pound test. Williams favored 6- or 8-pound test leader, usually about 12 feet long. He has caught thousands of salmon on the Miramichi, using hundreds of flies. He writes:

> My two favorite flies are the Black Dose and the Conrad. The Black Dose is a dark-bodied fly, sort of the opposite of the Silver Gray...When the water is up, I use a bigger hook, a double six or a double four, and, more than likely, flashier flies, like the Dusty Miller or Silver Cassaboom. The Butterfly is a showy fly with white wings that spread out and have a scissors action and a peacock body and brown hackle. You always need a showy fly in the spring when the water's high and moving hard.

COHO AND
CHINOOK SALMON

O to break loose, like the chinook

salmon jumping and falling back,

nosing up the impossible

stone and bone-crushing waterfall—

raw-jawed, weak-fleshed there,

stopped by ten steps of the roaring ladder, and then to

clear the top on the last try,

alive enough to spawn and die.

—Robert Lowell, from *Waking Early Sunday Morning*

COHO

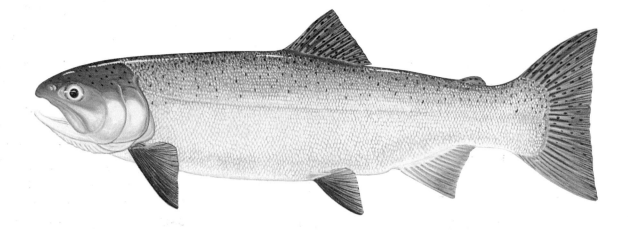

CHINOOK (Female)

While both of these Pacific species are pursued extensively by sportfishermen in saltwater, significant freshwater angling takes place in the Pacific freshwater estuaries and rivers where the coho and the chinook return to spawn—and most impressively in the Great Lakes, where the stocking of coho salmon has seen enormous success.

Range Cohos and chinook range throughout the Pacific Coast, from Washington to northern California. They now thrive in the Great Lakes. On the Pacific, cohos and chinook return to the rivers of their birth to spawn; in the Great Lakes the first-generation spawning salmon will initiate the freshwater rivers that will then become a permanent spawning ground.

Color The coho's upper body is bluish black and fades to silver on the flanks and white on the belly. Black spots appear on the back and upper part of the tail.

The chinook is generally a more muscular, broader fish than the coho, with a wider distribution of black spots and a darker-colored back.

Identifying characteristics The coho's mouth is usually gray or black, with whitish gums. The chi-nook's jaws feature a full complement of small teeth; the coho shows only a few.

Size The chinook grows larger than all other North American salmon and trout, commonly reaching sizes of 15 and 20 pounds by spawning time, and often weighing much more. Chinooks weighing 40 to 60 pounds are caught regularly throughout the Pacific Northwest. The IGFA all-tackle record is a 97-pound, 4-ounce chinook taken from the Kenai River, Alaska in 1985.

The coho peaks in a weight range between 10 and 15 pounds. The IGFA world record is a 33-pound, 4-ounce fish taken from the Salmon River, Pulaski, New York in 1989. Many 15- and 20-pound fish are caught, but very few between 20 and 30 pounds.

Spawning period Cohos spawn in the rivers where they were born during late fall and winter, entering fresh water in late summer. After birth, young cohos spend about a year in fresh water and then migrate to the sea, reaching adulthood at three or four years of age, at which time they turn for home and the arduous struggle

▲ *Coho fishing in Chugach National Forest.* ▶ *This river coho is making his final fight.*

to reproduce. The chinook spawns in the large freshwater rivers of the Northwest from June to November. Spawning cycles are complicated, occurring in some rivers every month of the year, with each run of salmon headed for one particular tributary or portion of the river's headwaters. Chinook fry take varying amounts of time to mature and migrate to sea, where they will forage vast stretches of ocean, growing at a rate of 3 to 6 pounds a year. After about five years of growth, the adults return to spawn, often traveling extraordinary distances. Tagged Pacific salmon have been known to travel up to 2,750 miles at an average speed of 40 miles a day. After spawning, all Pacific-grown salmon die.

The salmon's heroic struggle upriver against natural obstacles, predators, and the devices of man has inspired many articles, books, and poems. Every aspect of the salmon run is tinged with the nobility of unvanquished determination against nearly insurmountable odds. This passage from Roger Carras' *Sockeye* illustrates the point:

And the mathematics of it?
How do salmon numbers fare?
[A spawning adult] is one of
just 3600 fertile eggs that had
been placed in the gravel by
his mother and father. . .
Of the 3600, 106 smolt had
made it through the lake and as
far as the sea. Of those 106,
ten survived to reach the
mouth of the Coppertree System again. But there was the
final test, for of those ten,
eight would die in their

attempts to move upstream. Two of the more than 3600 eggs...would reach their natal bed and spawn.

In the Great Lakes, both cohos and chinook follow fall spawning migration patterns, entering the rivers of Michigan, Illinois, and New York in October and November. Mature fish caught early in the spawning cycle are top angling prizes, both for their fighting and eating qualities. Spinning and plug casting for spawning-run cohos in river inlets and shallows offer one of the most exciting and accessible sporting challenges in America.

Angling notes

On the Pacific Coast, the majority of coho and chinook fishing is done at sea from charter and private boats with herring downriggers. Further into the year, the salmon feed closer to the surface, and diving plane herring or anchovy rigs, crankbaits, and large, brightly colored spoons are all very effective. Once the salmon are found, they can most definitely be caught. When coho are feeding near the surface, enterprising Pacific Coast anglers tempt them with a streamer and fight the fish on a large fly rod—or work the moiling top water with plugs and spoons on light spinning gear. After cohos and chinook enter the great rivers of the Northwest—while leading salmon fresh waters once included the Columbia,

Running coho can be caught in huge numbers; professional angling captains can continue fishing through the season until the industry as a whole catches the maximum allowable number of fish, as determined by law.

Willamette, Skeena, Campbell, Sacramento, and Fraser rivers, coho and chinook populations are now down in nearly all of these, and some are threatened with extinction—a variety of angling methods may be employed to catch the homing salmon during their short days of travel to the spawning grounds. Drifting eggs or shrimp on Spin-n-Glo drift bobbers, mooching (or slow trolling), wet fly-fishing, and deep spinning are all popular methods.

In the Great Lakes, most salmon fishing is done from boats—except during the spring months, when foraging salmon can be caught in shallower water, and in October and November, when the spawning fish can be taken on flies and spinning lures in inlets and rivers. As the weather warms, the salmon seek out the thermocline, where the water is about 55°F and is rich with oxygen and schools of silvery minnows. Anglers and guides must locate schools in the thermocline with a depth probe and thermometer. Salmon can run as deep as 100 or 150 feet in the Great Lakes. The downriggers should be set to this depth, and herring or crankbaits strung behind the weight. Some favorite Great Lakes crankbaits include Rapalas, Rebels, and Tadpollies.

Fly-fishing

Chinook and cohos can be taken on the fly during spawning runs if anglers can present their streamers or wet flies where salmon are holding. Weighted streamers are best for deep-swimming Northwestern chinook. Brightly colored steelhead flies draw more results in muddy or milky water. Leaders should be short, hooks large, and fly-line backing very sufficient—at least 200 yards.

Best tackle

For trolling, use 20- to 30-pound test on a medium-size heavy trolling or heavy spinning reel, a fiberglass rod, and terminal tackle incorporating a 30-pound or so mono leader, flashers or dodgers to attract salmon schools, snelled hooks, and bait. For freshwater drifting, mooching, or noodling, long, fast, taper rods are the rule (noodle rods are especially long, thin, fast taper and are therefore sensitive), with 20- or 25-pound test line, 2-foot leaders, and pencil-weighted 1/0 or 2/0 hooks. For fly-fishing, 8- to 10-weight rods are essential, and for larger chinook, rods can go as high as 12 weight. Use sinking, weight-forward fly line, a short leader, and big hooks for chinook and smaller hooks for cohos.

Prize chinook or "king" salmon are sought after and often caught in the sounds and rivers of Alaska.

SHAD

AMERICAN SHAD

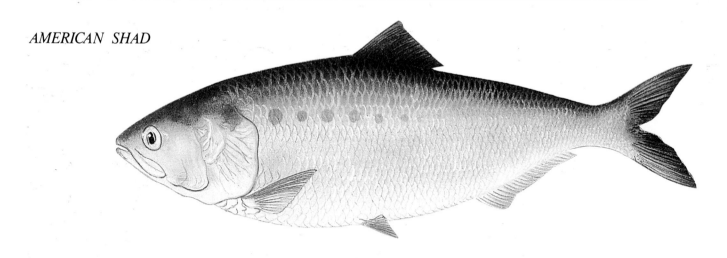

Range

Native to the Atlantic seaboard from Florida to the St. Lawrence River in Canada, both the *white* (also known as American shad) and *hickory shad* are anadromous fish that spend the majority of their lives in salt water but return to fresh water to spawn. In the 1870s, shad were successfully transplanted to the Pacific Coast and now flourish during spawning runs in fresh water from Alaska to southern California. During the middle part of this century, water pollution and river damming drastically curtailed shad spawning runs, and in some rivers the shad was completely cut off. But most of the shad's favorite rivers have been cleaned up, and special fish ladders give the shad right-of-way past gargantuan dams. The result? Teeming runs of shad that offer the anglers on both coasts accessible sport fishing.

Color

The back of the shad is green-gray with a metallic glint; its flanks and belly are silvery and its shoulders are marked with a line of progressively lighter spots.

Identifying characteristics

The jaw structures of the hickory and white shad tip off which species is which. The lower jaw of the white shad fits into a deep notch under the upper jaw, while the hickory shad's lower jaw protrudes noticeably beyond the upper jaw. All shad have full, plump bodies and swallow-forked tails.

Size

Shad average in weight between 3 and 6 pounds. From time to time, anglers hook into a 7- or 8-pounder. The world record shad, caught on the Connecticut River in 1986, weighed 11 pounds, 4 ounces. White shad live for about ten years and reach weights of 7 or 8 pounds. The hickory shad peaks at a smaller weight of about 5 pounds and prefers small tributary streams for spawning.

Often eager to strike, and very acrobatic, shad, "the poor man's salmon" make enormous runs up the Delaware and Connecticut Rivers, among others.

Spawning period

Shad leave the sea and begin their spawning run on both coasts in spring as the water begins to reach 60°F. In Florida, the shad begin to run during the first three months of the year. Mid-Atlantic fishermen wait until April or May before looking for shad. California runs begin in March.

Angling notes

Called "the poor man's salmon," the shad returns to fresh water after three or four years at sea. Little is known about shad migration, except that they feed voraciously en route to spawning grounds. Their appetite drives them to continue feeding as they enter fresh water, resulting in great action for anglers on both American coasts. The shad is absolutely unstoppable when it comes to hitting small flashing silver lures and offers the angler a very respectable round of fighting as it leaps and tail-walks to shake the lure. Shad migrate in staggering numbers that can mean dozens of strikes when they're on the feed; pools in the Delaware and Hudson rivers may hold thousands of fish during peak periods of the season.

Lures

Shad will hit any variety of silver or brightly colored lures, spoons, spinners, and jigs, as well as plenty of streamer flies and bucktails. Lures should be fished in the middle of the current or a *little* higher up, as shad rarely feed on the surface.

The "shad dart"—a small, tapered jig often fitted with a little colored buck-tail—is far and away the most popular lure. Small stream flies consisting of little more than a body of Mylar™ or tinsel and a few colored feathers are just as deadly. Other popular patterns

© Wendy Neefus/Earth Scenes

include the Enfile Shad Fly and the Chesapeake Bay Shad Fly. Flashy trout streamers—such as the Scarlet Ibis, White Marabou, and Yellow Sally—will take shad like they were born to them.

Best tackle

While it is true that shad fillets and roe are delicious, it is the acrobatic fighting power of the shad that makes it a valued game fish, and nothing will take the spunk out of a shad like heavy tackle. Light spinning gear or 5- or at most 6-weight fly line on a 8- to 9-foot rod will give the shad room to run, and allow even the minimally skilled angler to land the fish. In clear water, fly-rodders should use a long leader of at least 9 feet.

A boat is usually required to pursue deep-dwelling, cold water-seeking lakers.

© Greg L. Ryan/Sally A. Beyer

In spring and fall, lakers can be caught near shore as they move into shallower water. Here an angler tries his luck on Lake Superior.

tile again) means that the lake trout should be managed carefully, and the sportsman should return all but trophies and food to the water.

Angling notes

The lake trout is not a game fish for the angling masses. It mostly lives where it is damn cold, and to find the big specimens you've got to hitch up your dogsled and head for the tundra. Lake trout also often reside very deep in the water—sometimes 100 feet or more—although on cold and cloudy days large fish can be caught as they forage near the surface. A smart captain with trolling equipment can lead the lake trouter to some big, very aggressive fish, but smaller lake trout are uninspiring pugilists when compared to the steelhead or brown. A weekend spent pursuing lake trout will usually require a boat, depth finder, temperature probe, and a heavy-weight bait-casting rod and reel capable of trolling heavy flasher and herring rigs. Lead-core and wire line may be necessary to get the trolling rig down to the thermocline.

Lures

When trout are spotted in shallower water, the angler can cast to them with large, fluorescent-colored spoons like the Worth Demon, Johnson Minnow, Luhr-Jensen Super Duper Spoon, Les Davis Canadian Wonder, and Eppinger Husky Devel; heavy spinners; and deep-running blue, green, and silver-colored Rapalas and Rebels. Spoons and plugs are de rigueur for deep-water trolling with dodgers and flashers that can be combined with live bait.

Vertical jigging from a drifting boat will often catch lake trout. After dropping the jig to the bottom, you should retrieve it slowly and erratically, twitch-

ing it up and down as you work it toward the surface. If this doesn't raise much interest with the lakers, dress the jig with a strip of sucker or dead minnow.

Bait

Fishing 4- to 6-inch live smelts, suckers, or chubs near the bottom can draw freight-train strikes. Smelts, alewives, shiners, whitefish, perch, sculpins, or ciscoes are the preferred outrigging baits for trollers.

Best tackle

Boat trolling for lake trout requires sturdy bait-casting reels that cast 15- to 20-pound test. Also needed are short, 6- to 7-foot fiberglass downrigger rods.

All anglers owe themselves one long weekend catching lake trout in the forbidding wastelands of the Far North: Neither the fish nor the weather will be soon forgotten.

Diving plugs

RAINBOW TROUT
AND STEELHEAD

A real name—steelhead—rainbow

from the sea. He runs in summer, too,

but that is undramatic, the river

down and warm. No pour to push against.

No ice to snap his fins. No snow

to lay him on for photographs.

STEELHEAD (Female)

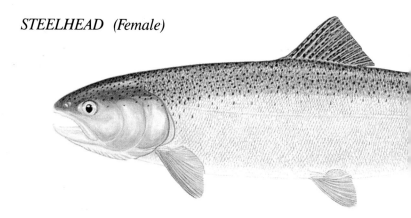

Men keep him warm with games. The steelhead

is a Burmese spy, a hired gun

from Crete. He comes to mate, not die

on some forgotten sand like salmon.

He rides the river out in spring

planning his drive for next December,

when big rains bring him

roaring from the sea with fins on fire.

—Richard Hugo, *Plunking the Skagit*

Range Able to tolerate great fluctuations in water temperature, the rainbow thrives in a great variety of waters, from the Aleutians to northern Mexico and in many selected eastern United States waters. Rainbows possess a strong anadromous instinct, and most coastal trout will migrate into the Atlantic and Pacific, where they will return to spawn as steelhead. Most steelhead (sea-run rainbow trout) are found in the coastal rivers of the West Coast, from northern California to Alaska. The steelhead rarely lives more than seven years, and ichthylogists denote the division between life in fresh water and salt water with a split age label—a rainbow that has spent one year as a smolt and parr in fresh water and two years as a fish at sea is recorded as 1/2 years old (one freshwater/two saltwater). A six-year-old fish that has lived two years in fresh water and four years in salt water is recorded as 2/4 years old.

Color The freshwater rainbow has a gray-blue upper body streaked with a broad, pinkish crimson stripe from head to tail. It is covered profusely with spots on the upper body and has a white belly. Col-

STEELHEAD (Male)

RAINBOW TROUT

oration varies tremendously among various rainbow hybrids, subspecies, and related species, which range from the Mexican golden trout to the Kern River golden trout. Gila trout, and Apache trout, all of which are so similar to rainbows biologically the ichthyologists have only recently come to an agreement on whether these various fish constitute separate or a single united species.

The steelhead's metallic bluish gray head and back brighten to shimmering silver on the flanks. It is also marked with a dash of black spots. As the steelhead remains in fresh water, it reverts to its original "rainbow" colors.

Identifying characteristics

The rainbow and steelhead both possess

Successful winter steelheading on Washington's Chief River.

a row of vomerine teeth on the roofs of their mouths, and their tails are slightly forked. The bodies and tails of both fish are liberally marked with prominent black spots, extending to the end of the tail, as opposed to the light tail spotting of the brown trout.

Size

Rainbows average 1 to 6 pounds in shallow waterways and grow even larger in the deeper, faster waters of the western United States and Canada. Lake rainbows grow the largest of the landlocked Mykiss (Onchorhynchus) species on their diet of large minnows, crayfish, and crustaceans. The IGFA record for freshwater rainbows is a 31-pound, 10-ounce giant from Lake Pend Oreille, Idaho in 1992. Steelhead weigh between 6 and 25 pounds, and some as large as 30 pounds have been caught on the fly rod. The all-tackle world record is a 42-pounder taken in Alaska. Steelies run in both summer and winter, with the winter fish running larger. Their size is determined by the number of years lived at sea, as the sea-run steelhead's high-fat, high-oil diet of squid, school fish, and small crustaceans continually adds muscle and heft. The energy spent in spawning will more or less equal the weight added during annual sea feeding, so the cumulative size effect of multiple spawning runs is nil.

Spawning period

No trout is as adaptable to poor or fluctuating water conditions as the rainbow, and no trout hybridizes so readily. While it prefers water between 45° and 65°F, it feeds actively in ranges significantly higher and lower than optimum. Rainbow hybrids have thrived in desert streams and rivers feeding the Gulf of Mexico, as well as in the icy waters of

This lovely rainbow was taken on Lily Lake in Colorado.

© Robert Pollock

Alaska and British Columbia. But all rainbow trout require fast-moving, highly oxygenated water for spawning, and stoked rainbows will not regenerate in slow waters.

Landlocked rainbows spawn from January to July, although cross breeding and the influence of hatchery fish has made it difficult to set any predictable patterns among large groups. Rainbows generally prefer water temperatures of around 55°F for spawning, although this can vary greatly by geographical area.

In the Pacific Northwest, steelhead return to spawn in summer, fall, and winter, homing in on their own river of birth. The spawning "window" is greatened or lessened by the turbulence or clarity of river conditions, and steelhead will run and spawn in smaller rivers within a few days if waters are low and clear. Not a schooling fish at sea, the steelhead's spawning runs

A freshwater rainbow is grafted on Long Lake in Minnesota.

reunite widely scattered individuals. Steelhead enter hundreds of Pacific Coast rivers, a number of which are famous for their fishing. These include the Deschutes and Oregon rivers in Oregon; the Klamath and Salmon in California; the Thorne and Karta in Alaska; the Dean, Campbell, and Chiliwack in British Columbia; the Washougal, Skagit, Skykomish, and Dungeness in Washington; and many, many others. Female steelhead use their tails to construct redds from gravel in shallow, cold, highly oxygenated water, and both males and females return to the sea after spawning. Few fish die naturally during the spawning cycle, though human and animal predation take their toll.

A handsome rainbow taken on the fly.

Angling notes   Both the landlocked rainbow and the steelhead offer fishing sport of exceptional quality. The rainbow is one of America's most popular sport fish. Youngsters and junior-fishing tournament teens ply eager hatchery rainbows with worms and dough balls, while serious fly-fishermen cast Skycomish Sunrises and Irresistibles to riffle-water 3-pound rainbows on the Deschutes in Oregon. A hardy and fast-growing trout in the wild, the rainbow's inclination to live in waters of varying temperature and purity—though it thrives in cold, clean, fast-moving water above all—makes it widely accessible to anglers across America. These same qualities offer appeal to hatchery operators, who prefer the highly adaptable rainbow for stocking. Hatchery stocking of rainbows throughout the East and Midwest has, despite its faults in promoting weak crossbreeds and forage competition,

largely preserved trout fishing in many parts of the country where it would not have survived. However, few pure-strain rainbow remain, and where they do exist in waters protected by falls, dams, or other natural or artificial barriers, they should be carefully managed by the sportsman and conservationist alike.

Steelhead is fishing for adults only. These sea-run trout return to their native rivers to spawn on both coasts in summer, fall, and best of all, in winter. Reluctant feeders, steelhead hold on the bottom of spawning rivers, where they must be fished precisely through a variety of bottom-dragging methods that are variously labeled plunking, mooching, noodling, and drifting. To catch steelhead, the right lure or bait must be presented at the right angle and drift or a strike is hopeless. It is difficult fishing, but what happens after the strike is extraordinary. The steelhead explodes into action, burning off 100 yards of line in an initial burst, tail-walking and leaping downstream in an all-out fight.

Lures In rivers, small bucktail spinners are productive on rainbows in late spring. Small floating diver plugs enjoy success, particularly with larger rainbows in the West. Try brightly colored spoons and spinners like the Luhr-Jensen Super Duper, Daredevel, Tiger Tail Spinner, Pixie Spoon, and Hot Shot Wobbler in deeper rivers for bigger fish.

Steelhead hold on river bottoms and will strike at lures as well as baits—the activity of the lures seems to irritate steelies into striking. A number of specialty methods have evolved for fishing these glittering warriors of the sea.

In *drift* fishing with lures and spinners, the steelhead angler must use pencil lead to get a lure to the river bottom, where it should drift with just enough line tension to create lure action against the current; usually a three-way swivel is used to connect the pencil lead, lure, and a small bobber that holds the lure just off the bottom. Often the float is brightly colored to suggest egg baits or simply draw predatory curiosity. The same principle is applied with live or natural baits, again rigged with floats or small "winged drifters"—a cross between a spinner and a float—to keep the bait in the steelhead's feeding zone (the Spin-n-Glo is a popular West Coast model of late). *Plunking* for steelhead means that sufficient weight is used to keep the bait or lure stationary; *drifting* means the whole bait bounces along with the river current, weighted to keep it low and rigged with a float to keep it moving. With steelhead, most anglers like to find out what lures have been working that season and try those first. Generally, lures are more productive when river waters are clear, baits when discolored; muddy conditions mean the steelie's sense of smell becomes more important in identifying food. Floating egg baits like Luhr-Jensen's Okie Bob and Gooey Bob are mainstays of Northwest fishing.

Noodling is fast becoming *très chic* among steelhead river fishermen. A noodle rod is taller than Kareem Abdul-Jabbar and designed to cast monofilament wispier than the floss he uses to clean his teeth. It is also extremely soft in taper, as in "limp as a noodle." This combination allows the steelhead angler to cast sensitive light test lines (noodlers in fact use 2- and 4-pound test) into the river with a springy rod that transmits the ghostly, faint taps and nibbles of the steelhead mouthing an egg or bait. The 14- and 16-foot lengths and the limpness of the blank help to protect light line from the strength and tenacity of the vigorous steelhead. While some fish are inevitably lost on the thready line, river noodlers claim to make far more hookups than other steelhead anglers.

In lakes, many anglers prefer trolling lazy Ike, Cotton Cordell, Rapala,

A typically huge steelhead taken on the customary steelie drift boat on the Hoh River in Oregon.

Rainbow

UNIT	METRIC EQUIVALENT
mile	1.609 kilometers
yard	0.9144 meters
foot	30.48 centimeters
inch	2.54 centimeters
ton	0.907 metric ton
pound	0.454 kilogram
ounce	28.350 grams

$$°F - 32 \times 5 \div 9 = °C$$

Silhouetted photographs

Courtesy Abel Automatics, Camarillo, CA: 81
Cabela's: 16, 41, 49, 63, *monofilament on 78,*
130; Lurh-Jensen: 25, 115, 125;
© Tony Cenicola: 28;
Courtesy Daiwa Corporation: 49, 66
Eppingers/Photo by Robert Jackson: 78